CULTIVATING CHAGA MUSHROOM MADE SIMPLE

A STEP BY STEP GUIDE TO CULTIVATING CHAGA MUSHROOM

DALTON FARMER

Table of Contents

CHAPTER ONE

Throughout the Northern Hemisphere, chaga mushrooms can be found attached to birch trees. It often looks like a dark clump of dirt, but upon closer inspection, it reveals bright orange tissue.

The chaga mushroom (Inonotus obliquus) has been shown to contain beneficial antioxidants and plant compounds.

Chaga is available as a herbal tea and supplement. Consuming chaga mushrooms as part of a healthy, balanced diet may help reduce oxidative stress, lower "bad" cholesterol, and support immune function.

This article takes a look at the research backing claims that chaga mushrooms are good for your health.

Many people believe the chaga mushroom, or Inonotus obliquus, can be used as a medicine because of its large size and dark color. Typically found on birch trees, Chaga mushrooms are native to the cooler northern regions of Asia, Europe, and North America.

The high melanin content in chaga causes its outer layer to darken dramatically when exposed to light, while the inner flesh retains its vibrant orange hue. When spotted in the wild, this mushroom might be mistaken for a clump of mud due to its extreme darkness.

Due to its bitter taste, Chaga is rarely consumed as a whole, but its use as a dried and powdered ingredient in beverages like coffee and tea has increased in recent years. The mushroom's purported ability to fight cancer and act as an antioxidant has led to extensive marketing. The powder is commonly sold as a nutritional supplement and is typically sold in pill form.

CHAPTER TWO

Facts About Nutrition

Chaga has many health-promoting components, such as high antioxidant levels and:

• B-complex vitamins

Vitamin D

• Potassium

• Rubidium

• Cesium

Amino acids

- Fiber

- Copper

- Selenium

- Zinc

- Iron

- Manganese

- Magnesium

- Calcium

Since the FDA doesn't regulate chaga, there is no readily available standard serving size or nutritional information.

The amount and type of chaga you consume will determine how many nutrients it provides per serving. Read the label and consult your doctor before beginning any supplementation with it.

Many people believe the chaga mushroom, or Inonotus obliquus, can be used as a medicine because of its large size and dark color. Typically found on birch trees, Chaga mushrooms are native to the cooler northern regions of Asia, Europe, and North America.

The high melanin content in chaga causes its outer layer to darken dramatically when exposed to light, while the inner flesh retains its vibrant orange hue. When spotted in the wild, this mushroom might be mistaken for a clump of mud due to its extreme darkness.

Due to its bitter taste, Chaga is rarely consumed as a whole, but its use as a dried and powdered ingredient in beverages like coffee and tea has increased in recent years. The mushroom's purported ability to fight cancer and act as an antioxidant has led to extensive marketing. The powder is commonly sold as a nutritional supplement and is typically sold in pill form.

Facts About Nutrition

Chaga has many health-promoting components, such as high antioxidant levels and:

• B-complex vitamins

Vitamin D

- Potassium

- Rubidium

- Cesium

Amino acids

- Fiber

- Copper

- Selenium

- Zinc

- Iron

- Manganese

- Magnesium

- Calcium

There's no standard serving size or nutrition information readily available for chaga, as it isn't regulated by the FDA.

The amount and type of chaga you consume will determine how many nutrients it provides per serving. Read the label and consult your doctor before beginning any supplementation with it.

Nutritional value

What exactly chaga mushrooms contain in terms of nutrients is unknown. However, they contain many helpful plant compounds and are high in antioxidants.

- triterpenoids

- melanins

- polysaccharides

- polyphenols

- flavans

People use chaga mushrooms not only as a supplement, but also in the preparation of teas and other infused beverages. Thus, chaga infusions do not typically have the same nutritional properties as whole mushrooms.

Eliminating LDL cholesterol

Numerous antioxidants and compounds can be found in chaga mushrooms, which may help lower LDL (bad cholesterol).

Chaga mushrooms may be helpful for lowering cholesterol, which reduces a major risk factor for cardiovascular disease.

Preventing and slowing cancer

A few investigations have looked into whether or not chaga mushrooms can thwart the development of cancer.

There are a lot of antioxidants in chaga. Antioxidants are substances that aid in protecting cells from free radical or oxidant damage.

When the body's natural antioxidant defenses are insufficient to prevent this damage, a condition known as "oxidative stress" develops. Oxidative stress has been linked to numerous diseases and disorders, including cancer.

Strengthening the Defense Mechanisms of the Immune System

Antigen-specific cytokines serve as chemical messengers in the immune system. White blood cells are the immune system's first line of defense against a wide variety of illnesses, and these proteins play a crucial role in stimulating them.

By facilitating intercellular communication, chaga may aid the immune system by regulating cytokine production. This has the potential to aid in the fight against infections of all severity levels.

Inflammation aids the immune system in its battle against disease. It's common for inflammation to be a temporary problem, but in some cases it can become chronic.

Inflammation has been linked to a number of diseases, particularly long-lasting ones like rheumatoid arthritis. Recent studies have shown that chronic inflammation may play a role in the development of many diseases and disorders, including some that are not traditionally thought of as inflammatory such as depression.

Chaga's role in regulating cytokine production may also help control inflammation.

CHAPTER THREE

Risks

As with other supplements and medications, chaga carries some risks. It's also possible for it to cause unpleasant side effects and have potentially lethal drug interactions with other treatments.

Because of its effect on blood sugar, chaga should be avoided by those who use insulin or similar medications.

Researchers have found that chaga extract in rodents can reduce platelet aggregation. The ability of a person's blood cells to clump together, known as platelet aggregation, is crucial for clotting. Therefore, it may have negative interactions with blood-thinning and blood-clotting medications.

Chaga mushroom users can minimize potential side effects by keeping in mind the following:

Keep taking all of your current meds, as chaga isn't meant to be a replacement for conventional treatment.

• Disclosing all medications to a healthcare provider. Chaga, like many other medicines and supplements, may interfere with the functioning of others.

• Keeping track of any adverse reactions to chaga. Chaga may cause a very slight allergic reaction in some people. Loss of consciousness, irregular heartbeat, and difficulty breathing all constitute medical emergencies.

If you're taking chaga on the advice of your doctor, you should not take any other herbal supplements at the same time.

Since the FDA does not regulate chaga, it is important to do research on supplement brands and only purchase from reputable retailers (FDA).

CHAPTER FOUR

See a medical professional before adding chaga mushrooms to one's diet. What daily dose of chaga is optimal for a given treatment must be individualized.

However, chaga should not be used in place of conventional medicine. People with chronic diseases like cancer, diabetes, or hypertension need to keep taking their medications as prescribed.

Only when advised to do so by a medical professional should chaga mushroom be used as a dietary supplement.

Summary

The antioxidant content of chaga mushrooms suggests they may have useful medical properties.

Some research suggests chaga mushrooms may help with things like lowering cholesterol, slowing cancer growth, bolstering the immune system, and lowering blood pressure, but this needs more investigation.

Mushrooms from the chaga genus can be found in numerous herbal teas and dietary supplements.

Some people may also experience side effects or an allergic reaction to chaga, so it's best to check with your doctor before taking any chaga supplements.

www.ingramcontent.com/pod-product-compliance
Lightning Source LLC
Chambersburg PA
CBHW050624160726
48003CB00003B/1319